Fearfully and Beautifully Made

My struggle with PMA (Progressive Muscle Atrophy)

Table of Contents

Preface

In this novel, I will tell you my true story about my struggles and my triumphs with God's help and how I managed to live with this disease, (a cousin to the ALS- Lou Gehrig's disease).

God chose this disease for me and I still don't know why, but I trust in him. Corinthians 10:13 says in the message "All you need to remember is that God will never let you down; he'll never let you be pushed past your limit; he'll always be there to help you come through it." This is the verse I hold onto when I feel desperate, depressed, or overwhelmed.

PMA is a rare form of MND (Motor neuron disease) that affects the nerves, which run from the spinal cord and controls your muscles, known as lower motor neurons. PMA results in muscles gradually losing their mass, known as atrophy or wasting. This causes the muscles to become weak, and a twitching sensation that ripples under the skin (known as fasciculation). It usually starts in the arms or legs and may only affect one part of the body for several years before spreading to other areas.

In this novel, I will tell you my true story about my struggles and my triumphs with God's help and how I managed to live with this disease, (a cousin to the ALS- Lou Gehrig's disease).

God chose this disease for me and I still don't know why, but I trust in him. Corinthians 10:13 says in the message "All you need to remember is that God will never let you down; he'll never let you be pushed past your limit; he'll always be there to help you come through it.". This is the verse I hold onto when I feel desperate, depressed, or overwhelmed.

PMA is a rare form of MND (Motor neuron disease) that affects the nerves, which run from the spinal cord and control your muscles, known as lower motor neurons. PMA results in muscles gradually losing their mass, known as atrophy or wasting. This causes the muscles to become weak, and a twitching sensation that ripples under the skin (known as fasciculation). It usually starts in the arms or legs and may only affect one part of the body for several years before spreading to other areas.

Fearfully and Beautifully Made My struggle with PMA (Progressive Muscle Atrophy)

Fearfully and Beautifully Made My struggle with PMA

(Progressive Muscle Atrophy)

Chapter 1–Background Information

I was born in Miami, Florida and moved to Naples Florida when I was four years old. My dad told my mom that he would not raise daughters in Miami. We did go to Miami every other weekend to visit our family there on my mom's side, who came from Cuba when Fidel took over. That story is for another book.

I had a wonderful childhood growing up. I had two wonderful parents and one sister; four years younger. I will preface my story by telling you that no one in my family has ever had any signs of ALS or any disease like mine.

Fearfully and Beautifully Made My struggle with PMA (Progressive Muscle Atrophy)

Fearfully and Beautifully Made My struggle with PMA
(Progressive Muscle Atrophy)

It was a beautiful summer day on the Fourth of July 1980. I was heading south to meet friends at a beach party. It was about 11 o'clock in the morning, on a clear day. Before I knew it, the person heading north turned left right in front of me without even using a signal. He was an older gentleman who said he did not see me. I never made it to the party. My car was totaled. There were no seat belt laws back then, and I went through the windshield. My forehead looked like hamburger meat. The plastic surgeon had to sand my forehead about eight times, one at a time until it healed. This process was repeated each time until the scars were gone. Here is a fact you may find interesting: there is no other skin on our body like our forehead skin. Grafting was out of the question. I tell you about this accident because I don't know if this is the reason, I have my disease. It's the only incident I've ever had that could have caused it. I wonder though, because my first symptoms didn't show up until 2013.

In 2013 I started having spasms in my left hand. It would send a pain up to my elbow and then go away after about 30 seconds. I dismissed it at first, thinking it was nothing. I found out later that the pain was nerve pain. I never thought it would be progressive muscle atrophy (PMA).

It took several years before I was finally diagnosed with PMA. I must admit I've had struggles with depression and frustrations because of the lost abilities of my hands, but I know that God is in control. When I asked the question why me, I hear a small voice saying, "why not you." I also prayed to be healed, and heard "no, you will be like Paul." In 2 Corinthians 12:8-9 Paul writes about his illness " Concerning this thing I pleaded with the Lord three times that it might depart from me. And He said to me, "My grace is sufficient for you, for My strength is made perfect in weakness."

This world is filled with disease and sorrow, but heaven is a place where we will forget all those things.

Chapter 2 The Diagnosis

In early 2014 I first went to my primary care doctor to see why I was having the spasms in my left hand. He sent me to a neurologist at Sharp, in San Diego. This doctor performed an EMG (nerve study) on me, and told me I had ALS – Lou Gehrig's disease. I had recently been proposed to by my boyfriend (now my husband). All I could think was I was going to die quickly; I told him he shouldn't marry me. He disagreed and told me he would never leave me. Today he still tells me he does not regret his decision. In fact he feels blessed by God to be with me.

After talking to some friends at work, I went to see a hand specialist at UCSD medical group. He ruled out ALS by looking at my tongue, of all things. He sent me to a shoulder and neck specialist first.

The shoulder/neck specialist ran an MRI on several parts of my neck and shoulder. She could not see anything, so I was referred to a neurologist at UCSD. The neurologist at UCSD also performed an EMG on me. He also sent me for several MRIs, and could not figure out what was wrong with me. The neurologist at UCSD moved to Scripps hospital and I continued to see him there until, I could not due to a health insurance policy change.

I went back to UCSD and asked to see a neurologist. I was told that the neurologist had to look at my file to see if he would want me as the patient. Luckily he did. I was told later it was because my disease is so rare. After more MRIs and more EMG's, he told me I had Hirayama disease.

Hirayama disease is a rare motor neuron disorder characterized by weakness and atrophy of the muscles of the hand and forearm. To this day, I could still have this disease since only my arms and hands are atrophying.

In October of 2016, however, my neurologist sent me to see a neurologist at Cedars-Sinai in Los Angeles for a second opinion. He diagnosed me with progressive muscle atrophy, and told me I would be alive to see my grandchildren, but he could not tell me what state I'd be in.

I was grateful to know what I had. Not knowing is very hard, The mind is so complex, and tends to look for a negative.
Research has shown that even a small amount of negative brain activity can lead to a weakened immune system, making you more prone to illness, and even lead to a heart attack or a stroke.

Negative attitudes can also affect your intelligence and ability to think. In fact, to choose gratitude we must meditate on it for 15 seconds, before it sticks.

Fearfully and Beautifully Made My struggle with PMA
(Progressive Muscle Atrophy)

Chapter 3- Daily Struggles

I'm very fortunate that this is a slow-moving disease which started in my left hand. Today, 2018, five years later, my left hand is completely atrophied to where it is unusable. It feels like it's broken. The disease is now affecting my right hand. I can no longer zip items, handle buttons, put on a coat or jacket, tie my shoes, etc. I also can't cut things with a knife or open any packages without scissors. I can only type with my pointer knuckle and the dragon software. This may sound as I can't do much anymore, but with God's help, I still seem to be able to quite a bit.

I can bathe myself, but not super good and can still dress myself; as long as I buy clothes that I can put on alone. I am able to tutor/ mentor at the Monarch school on Fridays, and can still hike and walk and cook to a certain extent. I do have stories to tell you about the struggles in the kitchen and how God comes to rescue me when I have no help at home.

Fearfully and Beautifully Made My struggle with PMA
(Progressive Muscle Atrophy)

Because of gravity, I am able to put things in the oven. When it's time for an item to come out, I struggle if it's hot or I no longer have the strength to lift it. On a few occasions my husband was late in coming home from work, and I was taking a casserole out thinking "it's going to burn even if I turn the oven off." I prayed to God to please give me the strength to pull the casserole out of the oven and I tried to do it with my weak right hand and my left hand that will not close. Guess what, I did it. It just goes to show you that with prayer, things that were not possible become possible.

Another time I was making chicken and biscuits in a cast-iron. That was hard to put in and take out of the oven. But with God's help I was able to. Don't misunderstand me, 97% of the time, I need assistance removing things from the oven.

I also struggle with brushing my hair. I must tell you I had long curly and course hair. It was knotted like crazy when I would get out of the shower. My husband would have to brush it for me, or I would end up with dreadlocks. I finally grew it out until I could donate it to the kids with cancer, and now I have short hair that I can manage on my own. I also thank the Lord for this.

These days, it's hard to pour from a quart of milk into my coffee, but again, with the Lord's help, most days I am able to manage.

Fearfully and Beautifully Made My struggle with PMA (Progressive Muscle Atrophy)

My husband is my greatest and favorite Angel. He does things for me every day; he cannot even imagine how much I appreciate him. Even though I say thank you for most everything, he can never understand the gratitude I feel towards him. I still can't believe that he chose to stay with me, knowing that I have this disease.

At work, my coworkers are always helping me. I can't open drawers. I can't remove staples, I can't pull files out of drawers, sometimes I can't even pick up a glass of water and definitely can't pour coffee from the coffee pot. It never fails, someone is always willing to help. Again, I am blessed to have a wonderful office to work in and to have such wonderful coworkers.

We went to Hawaii in May of 2018, and I had trouble snorkeling. I've always been a strong swimmer and was even a lifeguard when I was young. I can still tread water, but I can no longer do certain strokes with my arms. I am thankful I can do water aerobics in the pool, and with my husband's help, I can still snorkel.

In November 2018, we went to Naples Florida to meet the family for Thanksgiving. We have four kids together and everyone was there. It was such a blessing. We even found out we were going to be grandparents from our oldest son and his wife. During that trip, I could not open the doors to the house or car to save my life. With the help of all the people (family and friends) I was able to get into cars and out of the house. My family most definitely are God's angels on earth.

People help me daily. Sometimes at a gas station when I can't pump my gas. Other times at the grocery store when I can't pick up the juice. One day I was in sprouts and was trying to pick up apple juice for my neighbor, and it dropped three times, I just couldn't pick it up. A nice young lady with a little child offered to help me. Another one of God's angels helping me.

There was the time I went home sick with the flu going around. I stopped off a a restaurant for much needed chicken soup. It was raining. When I came out of the restaurant, I could not get the wet car door open, I couldn't get a grip on the handle. I tried and tried to open it and could not. I was starting to give up hope, and just then a yellow Hummer pulled up right next to me. An older man got out, and I asked him if you could please help me. He came over and opened the door and also closed the door for me. You guessed it, another one of God's Angels on earth helping me. I truly believe that there are Angels here on earth.

This disease is bringing me closer to the Lord. I can no longer depend on my own strength. The other day in church we were singing God, I need you every hour, and I was singing God, I need you every minute. It made me cry. The devil is never far from trying to make my life more difficult, but when I cry out and pray to God, a peace comes over me that I cannot explain.

Most nights, I get nerve pain when I try to sleep. It attacks my thighs, my legs, and my feet. I was dreading sleeping. I went to the doctor and got medicine for it, and nothing worked. My son told me about CBD oil. He ordered me some from Charlotte's Web, and that stuff worked like nothing ever before. When I take it, I don't get nerve pain in my legs, thighs, or feet and sleep peacefully. I am so thankful that my son turned me onto this medicine.

Recently, I began having trouble opening the car door and with the gear shift. My husband went to Home Depot and bought some long zip ties. He looped one around the door handle and took another smaller one and tied it around the gear shift. It works like a charm. I am so grateful for him and all he does for me.

Fearfully and Beautifully Made My struggle with PMA
(Progressive Muscle Atrophy)

I am very lucky I have this disease today and not twenty years ago. Technology is helping me immensely. I can still work with the help of Dragon software and a speaker. New Ziploc bags with sliders and door locks with combinations instead of key, cars that are keyless, all of these things are helping me today. I am definitely thankful for all the things the Lord has helped me with, technology and people.

In January 2019 I started having trouble grocery shopping. In fact at Sprouts, 2 different customers helped me pick up things I was struggling with. Other times, co-workers go with me and help me.

Fearfully and Beautifully Made My struggle with PMA (Progressive Muscle Atrophy)

Chapter 4 Work and What's Next

I am still working, and with the help of the Dragon software and a Bluetooth speaker I am able to still do the accounting work at my job. I don't know how much longer this will last, as I still need to use my hands to a certain extent. But I trust God to let me know when it's time to go out on disability. I am very lucky to work where I work. I was a consultant with the organization until I found out I was going to need disability.

I asked the Executive Director to consider hiring me because of the situation. He agreed and put me on payroll with disability insurance. I feel very thankful knowing that I will be able to continue to contribute to our finances even if I can't work.

People worry that I'll be more depressed once I do go out on disability, but I know that with God's help I will continue to do his will. I plan to tutor at the Monarch school more than just once a week. I find that working out also helps me control my depression. When I don't go, I feel the depression more, but the serotonin that we receive once we work out pulls me out of the depression.

One day a thought came into my head, which I must give credit to God for. He sent me to find some college students to help me with my daily struggles. God does work in mysterious ways. Later that week I called the college Point Loma Nazarene and was told that they could not help me in that I should talk to my church.

We were invited over to a friend's house for dinner. Gresham and Deidre Bayne are people we met thru Jane Howard. As we were talking, they found out I have an MBA. Gresham invited me to have lunch with the girl he mentors.

I met Bailey Holmes that day. She was studying to get her MBA at Point Loma Nazarene. After the discussion of what was said she offered to post my job on the Point Loma Nazarene Facebook page. A week later I had six girls emailing me to help me. God is truly amazing. He has brought me Tori and Becca, two freshmen girls from Point Loma Nazarene. They have been amazing, positive and great helpers. Our friendship is growing and my love for them is growing as well. They are amazing girls, and I hope to mentor them and guide them spiritually. They are willing to do anything I ask, and to be my hands for me. This means so much to me. It also means I don't have to burden my husband with the daily chores. They say I am blessing them, and I say they are blessing me.

Me with Tori

Me with Becca

In January 2019, we had Joel's daughter Robyn get married. It was such a lovely wedding. Joel's mother came (who is like a mother to me) , and both of our families were in attendance. It was a beautiful wedding, and we love our new son in law. The whole family were offering me help during the festivities.

In March 2019. We went to our house in Florida to start working on renovations. God was so present in our lives. It was amazing. Home Depot has sent out a design person for the kitchen, and he gave me his computer with pro-referrals through Home Depot to log into. We found two Venezuelans a father-son team to help us. They came over the same day in afternoon and started working. The next day we went to look at granite and tile for the floors, and they gave us more names of people who told us about other people to help us. Our next-door neighbor gave us the name of the window and door vendor, who we went to visit. It felt like dominoes falling in place. By the time we were leaving, all the walls were fixed, the drywall was repaired, the popcorn ceiling had been removed and the texture on the ceiling was being done. Two weeks after we left, the flooring tile was installed.

We never imagined that we would get so much done in a week, we even found a couch that reclines that is touch, so I can even do it with my weak hand. I give all the glory to God. With his help, anything is possible. God provides for me every day. My friend told me her mom uses the term "mm" for mini miracles. I love it. If you look, you will see mm's in your life too.

The summer of 2019 was a busy one. In May, we went to the island of Oahu, Hawaii. We had a wonderful time. We went to Pearl Harbor and Hanauma Bay. We hiked Diamondhead crater and stayed on the north shore for 3 days. We had a great time, and with my husband's help, I was able to do it all.

In June, we had several blessings. We were blessed with our first granddaughter, Joel threw me a surprise party, we went to Florida to work on the house and went to a Padre game with our preacher and her family. It was a memorable month.

Padre game

We were blessed with our first grandchild on June 25th. Her name is Evelyn Grace and she is a beautiful miracle. She is so special to us. We planned to visit her and booked a flight before she was born for the end of June. She was late and we were there three days after her birth. The love we have for a baby, such unconditional love, reminds me of God's love for us. In 1John 4:16 "So we and rely on the love God has for us. God is love. Whoever lives in love, lives in God, and God in them."

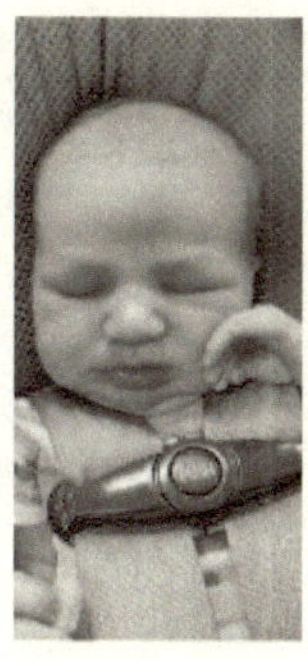

My birthday was in June and Joel threw me a surprise party. He enlisted my friends to help him. I was completely surprised, I had no clue. I had been asking to go away for it and Joel kept saying no. I was getting a bit upset. To my dismay, he took me to the pool area in our condo (we used it as a cut through) and there were my friends. I started to cry,and felt awful for hounding Joel. It all became clear. It was a blast. He is truly the best husband ever. All my friends are so special too, always willing to help.

July and August were eventful as well. We had family visit for the 4th of July, we went to visit Joel's mom in Texas, and I went on long term disability at the end of August.

Robyn and Bryce flew out for the 4th of July. We had a nice time and saw the fireworks on our neighbor Jane's deck. Jane is 96 years old, but you'd never know it. She is front and center in my birthday picture. She is definitely one of God's Angels.

During that visit, Robyn told me about electrolysis as something I should look into, since I could no longer shave. I looked into it and found a Groupon for a place in La Mesa called "Bare Skin Beauty" I met Stella, the owner, a kind, compassionate and

Fearfully and Beautifully Made My struggle with PMA
(Progressive Muscle Atrophy)

Godly woman, who I am working with to remove permanently the hair on my legs. She uses an electrical current to remove one hair at a time. While it is painful, I am hopeful it will work. She and I have become friends, and I am very grateful for her.

Joel lost his father in 2018, a grief I know (I lost my dad in 2012 and my mom in 2013). We try to visit his mom, who has trouble walking, as often as we can. I always enjoy her company, and we laugh so much, We joke, we are two handicap people helping each other. She is also one of God's Angels.

Chapter 5: Retirement

My disease has moved to my right hand (it took 3 years) and I can no longer fill a printer with paper, pull files, and have lost the ability to use a pen or pencil to write. These things were important in my job. I decided it was time to go on disability. The staff at work threw me a party, and were sad to see me go, as was I. I loved my co-workers and I as lucky to have a wonderful boss.

My last day was on August 31st, 2019. I was worried I would be depressed, but with the holidays approaching, our new granddaughter, packing for the move, bible study and writing this book and electrolysis, I had no time to become depressed. I am so thankful for these things.

We were lucky to babysit our grandchild for two weeks in November. I must admit it was hard for me to not be able to pick her up, dress her, feed her or put her down for a nap. I did find joy however, by singing and dancing for her and reading and playing with her. I can't express the love and joy I have for her. It is beyond words.

We had our family here for Christmas, and the college girls helped me decorate. My sister helped fix breakfast meals for me, as I can no longer close my hands. I made reservations for Christmas eve and Christmas day dinner, to make things less stressful.

Before the holidays, the girls helped me make cookie dough, and we froze it, and my neighbor Pam helped me make toffee. They 'were all a big hit. Jane went to visit her daughter for Christmas, and let us use her place. That was a "mm". She has a beautiful place, and it allowed us to all be together.

I recently found out only 200 people in the world have my disease. I realize most people with PMA lose the ability to walk first (their feet flop). I have yet to hear or see about anyone who has lost the use of their hands. I am so grateful for this. I know God chose me, to give me this disease, and I consider it a gift. I feel it is so my light would shine, and bring others to him. I know my suffering is helping me grow closer to God. The bible says : "We know that suffering produces perseverance; 4 perseverance, character; and character, hope. 5 And hope does not put us to shame, because God's love has been poured out into our hearts through the Holy Spirit, who has been given to us."(Romans 5:3-5).

Fearfully and Beautifully Made My struggle with PMA
(Progressive Muscle Atrophy)

I can no longer close my hands, and now my right leg is getting weak. I can no longer climb stairs with my it. In fact, I recently tried and fell backwards, hitting the back of my head. I was not hurt, yet another "mm".

Feeling discouraged, I decided to read Nick Vujicic's book "Life without Limits" It was a testament to God's faithfulness. A man born with no arms or legs, has a smile on his face, and a full life with a wife and children. He travels all over the world, trying to help others. If I compare myself to him, I am fine.

After reading his book, I decided to look up how people with no arms function. What I found, has changed my life. It never would have occurred to me, they use their feet. On YouTube, I watched people drive, eat, and do even more with their feet.
I now use my feet to open drawers, the crisper drawers in the refrigerator, the front loading washer, cabinets and more. My feet help me with anything my hands can't open because they are weak and won't close.

Fearfully and Beautifully Made My struggle with PMA (Progressive Muscle Atrophy)

40

Chapter 6- Conclusion

Whatever you are going through, please take heart. Know that God is with you, and will never give you more than you can handle. The bible says: "We know that God is always at work for the good of everyone who loves him" (Romans 8:28).

My disease is an insidious one as it robs me of use of my body daily, but thank God it has not limited my mind. I choose to continue to have faith in God, and trust in him. Don't get me wrong, we all walk through peaks and valleys, whether disabled or not, but if you trust in the One who created you, you will be able get through it, with his help.

This disease is not easy to live with. We all must make a choice on what will do when we wake up in the morning. We can choose to have a positive outlook or a negative one. I choose to be thankful for the breadth I breath and for another day. When I think about those less fortunate than me, I feel like I have nothing to complain about. I hope you will too.

Fearfully and Beautifully Made My struggle with PMA (Progressive Muscle Atrophy)

Whatever you are going through, please take heart. Know that God is with you, and will never give you more than you can handle. The bible says: "We know that God is always at work for the good of everyone who loves him" (Romans 8:28).

My disease is an insidious one as it robs me of use of my body daily, but thank God it has not limited my mind. I choose to continue to have faith in God, and trust in him. Don't get me wrong, we all walk through peaks and valleys, whether disabled or not, but if you trust in the One who created you, you will be able get through it, with his help.

This disease is not easy to live with. We all must make a choice on what will do when we wake up in the morning. We can choose to have a positive outlook or a negative one. I choose to be thankful for the breadth I breath and for another day. When I think about those less fortunate than me, I feel like I have nothing to complain about. I hope you will too.